W9-AGB-535

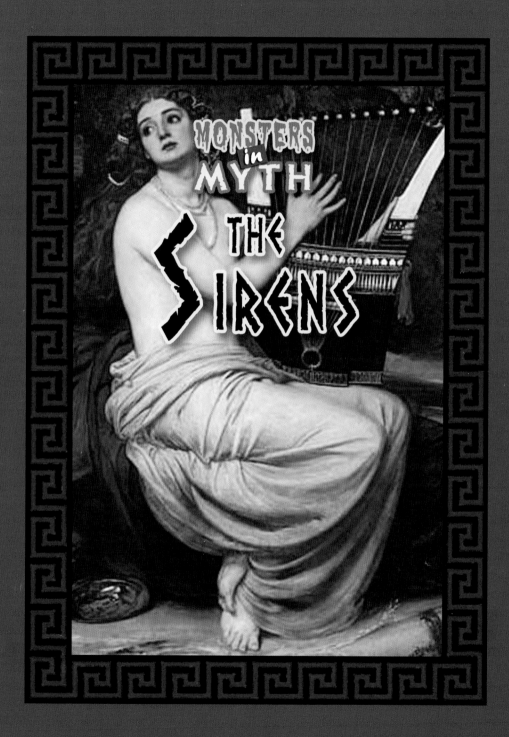

MONSTERS in MYTH

THE Sirens

MONSTERS in MYTH

TITLES IN THE SERIES

MONSTERS in MYTH

THE SIRENS

TAMRA ORR

Mitchell Lane
PUBLISHERS

P.O. BOX 196
HOCKESSIN, DELAWARE 19707
VISIT US ON THE WEB: WWW.MITCHELLLANE.COM
COMMENTS? EMAIL US: MITCHELLLANE@MITCHELLLANE.COM

PUBLISHERS

Printing   1   2   3   4   5   6   7   8   9

Library of Congress Cataloging-in-Publication Data
Orr, Tamra.
  The sirens / by Tamra Orr.
      p. cm. — (Monsters in myth)
  Includes bibliographical references (p.   ) and index.
  ISBN 978-1-58415-930-8 (library bound)
  1. Sirens (Mythology)—Juvenile literature. I. Title.
  BL820.S5O77 2011
  398.20938'01—dc22
                                                                2010026965

ABOUT THE AUTHOR: Tamra Orr is the author of more than 250 nonfiction books for readers of all ages, including *The Monsters of Hercules* for Mitchell Lane Publishers. Several of her books have won awards, including the New York Public Library Best Nonfiction Book for Teens and Youth Advocates Honorable Mention. Orr lives in the Pacific Northwest with her children, husband, cat, and dog, and in her spare time she reads about gods, heroes, and monsters of the ancient Greek world.

AUTHOR'S NOTE: The stories retold in this book use dialogue as an aid to readability. The dialogue is based on the author's extensive research. Documentation of such research is contained on page 45.

PUBLISHER'S NOTE: The internet sites referenced herein were active as of the publication date. Due to the fleeting nature of some web sites, we cannot guarantee they will all be active when you are reading this book.
    To reflect current usage, we have chosen to use the secular era designations BCE ("before the common era") and CE ("of the common era") instead of the traditional designations BC ("before Christ") and AD (*anno Domini,* "in the year of the Lord").

TABLE OF CONTENTS

MONSTERS IN MYTH

THE SIRENS

The Siren, by John William Waterhouse, 1900. The Sirens sent their lovely voices across the waves to bait sailors. They reeled them in with harmony and before the men knew it, they were trapped forever.

CHAPTER 1

Facing the Siren Song

We looked out to sea as we did every day, hoping to spy a mast on the horizon. We scanned the cloudless blue sky in search of a sail and turned our ears toward the waves to listen for the sound of men approaching. At last, a ship appeared and we all smiled at each other, knowing it was time to cast our voices across the water and lure the men in with bait made of harmony.

But what was this? The ship belonged to Odysseus (oh-DIH-see-us), the one of whom we had heard so many tales. He had fought at Troy and was on his weary journey home. He had escaped the Lotus-eaters, blinded the Cyclops (SY-klops), and gotten away from the Laestrygonians (ly-struh-GOH-nee-uns), a race of cannibals. He had even survived a journey to the Underworld. How could we possibly add to his troubles?

It was our duty. With great sadness, we began to sing. As we expected, when the wind carried the notes across the ocean, Odysseus began to thrash and scream with longing to come near us. Wait—he was tied to the ship's mast and couldn't escape. What of his men? They acted as if they did not even hear us. How could that be? Was our power suddenly gone? No, it was that evil Circe! She gave away our secret and so, somehow, these men could block out the sound of our song. Sing harder, my sisters. Perhaps we can at least drive Odysseus mad before he sails too far!

Temptation Ahead

Odysseus shivered and moaned. He begged his men for relief. He pleaded, bribing them with whatever he could think of for rescue. It was all in vain. His men turned their backs to his agony. They could not hear his pleas; they closed their eyes against his bribes. Odysseus cried out with misery, but there was no help forthcoming. His punishment continued, made worse by the fact that he knew he was the one who had ordered it.

Odysseus was not easily conquered or bowed. He was brave and strong. He lived for adventure, and in fact epic poems and stories would be written about his daring encounters with hideous monsters and angry enemies. He survived the temptations of the sneaky Lotus-eaters, who lured sailors in with plants that drugged them and made them forget about their homes. He escaped from the man-eating Cyclops, thanks to his cunning.

Then his ships sailed to the Aeaean Island of Circe (SIR-see, or KEER-kee), where Odysseus encountered an entirely different kind of danger. Circe, daughter of Helios (HEE-lee-ohs) the sun god, ruled the island. She was a powerful magician. After baiting sailors with food and wine, she turned many of them into wolves, lions, and other animals. She turned Odysseus's men into swine and tossed them into cages. Odysseus discovered what had happened and was determined to rescue them. On his way to try to convince Circe to let them go, he was approached by the god Hermes. He handed Odysseus a magical herb that he promised would protect him from Circe's spells. Odysseus ate it and hurried to meet the evil sorceress.

Just as before, Circe lured her new visitor in with offers of food, wine, and rest. When the time came to turn him into an animal, however, she discovered her spell did not work. Instead of transforming into a four-legged creature, Odysseus charged her, sword in hand. Circe fell to her knees, begging for mercy. Odysseus offered her a deal: return all of his men to human form and let them go on their way without any further magic, and he wouldn't kill her. She agreed, and surprisingly, she kept her word.

In Book 10 of *The Iliad*, Odysseus describes the experience:

Circe Offering the Cup to Ulysses, John William Waterhouse, 1891. Circe was used to getting what she wanted. She offered her magical cup to Odysseus (whom the Romans called Ulysses), but the spell did not work.

> Circe walked on out through the hall, staff in hand,
> and opening the doors of the pigsty she drove them
> out, looking like nine-year-old hogs. They stood facing
> her, and she went among them, anointing each of them
> with some other drug. The bristles, grown on them
> from the harmful drug that Circe had supplied, fell
> away from them and they turned once more into men,
> but younger and taller and handsomer than before.[1]

In the following days, Odysseus and his crew were treated with the greatest care. They had whatever they wanted, and in return, they shared the tales of their many great adventures before reaching Circe's island. Time passed, and soon a year had gone by. Finally, they decided it was time to return to the sea and head home. Circe agreed and did them one more favor. She told them of the dangers that stood between them and home. Although her warnings frightened the men, Odysseus was determined to return to his wife and family in Ithaca. No sea monsters or other threats were going to stop him.

A Warning

The first danger they would face, said Circe, was a group of women known as the Sirens. They had killed many sailors already, enticing them with their music and then watching as either the ships crashed on the rocks around their island or the men leaped into the raging sea to drown. Circe explained, in Book 12 of *The Iliad*,

> First you will reach the Sirens who enchant all men,
> whoever comes their way. Anyone coming near,
> not knowing, and hearing the Sirens singing, never
> will he go home to his wife and little children,
> never will they delight in his return, but the Sirens
> enchant him with the sweetness of their singing,

sitting in their meadow, with all around them
a great heap of bones from men rotting away
whose skins wither upon them . . .[2]

The men tried to imagine what the sound of the Sirens must be like. How could women's voices and music be so enchanting as to make men forget their loved ones and their homes? How could they

Ulysses and the Sirens, Herbert James Draper, 1909. In some versions of the myth, the Sirens did not wait for sailors to come to them and instead invaded their ships. They stormed the ship of Odysseus (Ulysses), hoping to grab the famous adventurer.

abandon their ship, their duties, and their friends just to follow the sound of a flute, a lyre, or a voice, no matter how lovely? Odysseus was determined to find out—but he wouldn't allow his men to.

Once the crew set sail and were dangerously close to the Sirens' islands, Odysseus was visited by a talking bee, who offered the men a ball of beeswax to place in their ears. This way no sound could get through. Odysseus ordered his men to comply, but he refused to use the wax. He had to hear the Sirens' song. He had his men lash him tightly to the mainmast of the ship and told them that no matter what he said or did, they were not to untie him. He was to stay bound until the ship had sailed out of the Sirens' reach.

His men followed his orders, but now Odysseus was desperate. He heard the sound of these mysterious women, and even though he could not see them on the faraway shore, he knew they had to be beautiful. He wanted to go to them. Their songs promised to reveal the world's greatest secrets to him. All truth and knowledge would be shown to him if only he would leap off his ship and swim to their island. He wanted to go!

Odysseus continued to struggle against the ropes, tempted by the Sirens' song. He pulled and tugged but the ropes only got tighter. His men restrained him, and ever so slowly, his ship moved beyond the sound of the Sirens. Finally, their music was not even a whisper on the wind. The men took the wax from their ears, and at last they untied their leader. The ship and its crew continued their dangerous journey home.

What happened to the Sirens? Some legends say that they, in despair because someone had heard their song and lived to tell about it, threw themselves into the sea to drown. Other stories report that they were transformed into rocks. No matter how they reached their end, one thing is sure: the Sirens were wicked women who haunted sailors' dreams and brought an end to many young men's lives.

The Tales of Odysseus

Few names are as familiar as Odysseus in the world of literature, primarily because the blind poet Homer told of the hero's exciting adventures in both *The Iliad* and *The Odyssey*. Also known as Ulysses (yoo-LIH-seez, the Latin version of his name), Odysseus is considered one of the greatest leaders in all of mythology. He was known for his cunning and intelligence—which he frequently used to get out of whatever trouble he found himself in.

During the Trojan War, Odysseus fought bravely. He, with the help of Athena, came up with the idea of the Trojan Horse, a strategy that allowed Greek soldiers to sneak into the city of Troy and conquer it. After the death of Achilles (ah-KIH-leez), Odysseus was the one to win the fallen soldier's respected armor.

The tale of Odysseus's ten-year journey from Troy to his home in Ithaca is full of adventure. In addition to facing the Lotus-eaters, the Cyclops, Circe, and the Sirens, he also traveled in the Underworld and survived multiple shipwrecks (the result of angering the sea god, Poseidon).

Once Odysseus returned home, life was still challenging. During the twenty years he was gone, his wife, Penelope, had been under tremendous pressure to remarry. Not only were men waiting in line to become her new husband, but they had moved into her home and were eating her food, drinking her wine, and behaving rudely to her and her son Telemachus (teh-LEH-muh-kus). When Odysseus found out what was going on, he put on the disguise of a beggar and, with the help of friends, fought and killed all of the suitors. It took several battles, but at last, Odysseus was home with his family—and with hours and hours of tales to tell.

Return of Odysseus, by Nicholas Monsiau, early 1800s. After so many years, Odysseus' exciting return was full of challenges.

In an Attic vase painting dating back to the sixth century BCE, Athena and Poseidon argue over which of them would be a better protector of Athens.

CHAPTER 2

An Ongoing Feud

Where did the Sirens come from? As with other Greek and Roman myths, there are different stories to explain their beginnings. If you read all of these stories, you will find some contradictions. In mythology, time frames do not always match up, and the characters are not always the same.

A Family Feud

One of the main stories about the Sirens centers on a feud between Athena (ah-THEE-nuh), the goddess of wisdom and daughter of Zeus (ZOOS), and Poseidon (poh-SY-dun), the brother of Zeus and god of the sea. Athena and Poseidon were simply not able to get along.

In order to keep harmony on Olympus, the mountain where the gods dwelled, Zeus had decided that he did not want any of the gods or goddesses arguing with each other. If they did, they would be punished. Although it was a good idea in theory, it was not an easy rule to enforce. Many of the gods and goddesses had quick tempers. Some were jealous and conceited; others were moody and greedy. Athena was driven by envy, and Poseidon expected—demanded— worship from all people.

Athena had had enough of Poseidon. As commander of the sea, he had far too much power, in her opinion. He kept sailors and captains in mortal fear of rough seas, sharp rocks, and threatening sea monsters. He insisted that fishermen sacrifice to him in order to harvest their nets of fish, and he frightened those living on the coast with unpredictable storms and damaging floods. Athena wanted to lessen Poseidon's power. She came up with a devious plan, and she knew just whose help she needed to carry it out.

15

The Shape Shifter

Poseidon, known to the Romans as Neptune, had two sons: Triton (TRY-tun) and Proteus (PROH-tee-us). Proteus had a remarkable talent. He could change into the shape of whatever creature he wanted to. He worked for his father, but one day he was summoned to see the goddess Athena. He was suspicious—and he had good reason to be. Athena promised Proteus great wisdom if he would help humble Poseidon. Proteus said no thank you. A little knowledge was simply not payment enough for him to betray his father.

When he refused, Athena was not happy. She decided he needed more convincing. She knew that he could transform himself only four times in a row before permanently becoming a sea blob, as he was born. She asked him to transform for her, and he was flattered. He changed to a sea blob, but when he felt Athena's hands begin to squeeze the life out of him, he quickly turned into an eel. She did not let go! Her strong hands kept squeezing. Next, he turned into a bull and tried to stab her with his horns, but before he could, she grabbed a magical thread from her loom and tied him up.

Finally, Proteus turned into a tiger—his fourth transformation— and reached for Athena with his sharp claws and teeth. Before he could harm her, she captured and trapped him. He had no choice but to return to being a sea blob. She then made her plan very clear. If he did not help her, she was going to pound him into jelly! Then she would take the jelly and spread it on others so that they could transform into other creatures. Proteus swore he would help her if she would only let him live.

Making a Deal

Athena told Proteus exactly what he was to do: Go to Circe and teach her the art of transformation. Proteus was also to choose two sea nymphs to take with him and teach as well. Once these women understood how to change themselves at will, they would be given the task of wrecking ships, killing sailors, destroying fish harvests,

For a moment, Proteus was a powerful tiger—but Athena still did not release him.

and generally causing so much trouble at sea that people would stop worshiping Poseidon and turn against him.

In fear for his life, Proteus cooperated. He went to Circe's island, picking up two sea nymphs on the way. They were sisters named Teles (TEE-lees) and Ligeia (ly-GEE-uh). He taught them and Circe the art of transformation, and they were quick learners. However, while they all liked Proteus, there was a growing tension between Circe and the two nymphs. Circe felt that she should be treated as a

Circe Invidiosa (Jealous Circe), John William Waterhouse, 1892. Circe knew how to make potions and spells from many things, including water. Her sorcery created trouble for many sailors.

goddess—but the other women didn't agree. Bickering began. It turned into arguments. Proteus knew the only solution was to separate the women. He told Circe to stay on shore and turn shipwrecked sailors into animals. He instructed the sisters to build fires on the edge of the shore to lure in ships.

It was as if Poseidon was listening to his plans as he made them. Every time the sisters built a fire, he sent rain to put it out. Proteus had to come up with another idea.

He decided that the nymphs should sit on the rocks and sing to lure in travelers. Although they already had beautiful voices, he trained them even more until they were irresistible when they sang. The plan worked. The sisters brought the ships in close enough to splinter and sink on the rocks. Any survivors who made it to shore would find Circe, who turned them into animals.

The Ones Who Got Away

Athena was happy. Her plan to discredit Poseidon was working. Proteus was happy. He had done what he was supposed to and was allowed to go free without harm. Circe was happy. She had a palace full of food.

The sisters, however, were not happy. They felt bad about luring the sailors to either death or life spent as a caged animal. One day, a ship wrecked, and two of the sailors, Pero (PAYR-oh) and Procles (PROH-kleez), made it to shore but did not follow the rest of the crew to Circe's palace. Instead, they stayed with Teles and Ligeia. The women sang to the men; the men told the sisters adventure stories. When Pero and Procles fell asleep, the women carried them into Circe's castle and, using their spells, turned the men into a monkey and a cat.

Hiding in a tree high above was an owl, a spy for Circe and Athena. When it saw what the sisters had done, it flew to Circe and reported them. In a rage, she ran to the sisters and cast a spell to turn them into birds. She was so upset, however, that she made a mistake, and Teles and Ligeia were given wings only. Seeing their chance to escape, they flew to a nearby set of islands.

Although the sisters thought they must be free, it was not quite true. Their voices were even lovelier now that they were part bird. When they sang, they lured in more sailors than ever. Athena was pleased, but she feared that the sisters would have soft hearts and rescue more men than they killed. To make sure this didn't happen, she placed a vicious, man-eating jellyfish in the waters around the island. It would take a clever and brave sailor named Butes (BOO-teez) to solve that problem.

The man-eating jellyfish. Jellyfish like this one may look beautiful, but often a single touch is enough to wound—or, in some cases, kill—a person.

God of the Sea

Poseidon was worshiped mainly because he was so feared. If he liked you and was in a good mood, he might lull you to sleep on soft waves and under calm skies. However, if he didn't like you or you'd done something to irritate him, he could be cruel—or fatal.

In his epic poems, Homer paints word portraits of the god that show both sides: the gentle, peaceful one and the violent, dangerous one. In *The Iliad*, he wrote:

> He harnesses to his chariot his two bronze-shod horses,
> swift of foot, with long, streaming manes of gold.
> Himself clothed in gold, he seized his well-wrought
> golden whip, then climbing into his chariot he drove
> across the waves. On every side, from the deeps of the sea,
> came dolphins, playing in his path, acknowledging his lord,
> and the sea parted in joy, cleaving a path before him.
> So swiftly sped the horses that never once
> was the axle of bronze beneath made wet with foam.[1]

Later, in *The Odyssey*, he described the other side of Poseidon:

> He drew the clouds together and grasping his trident
> he stirred up the sea. He roused the storm blasts
> of all the winds together, and covered with clouds
> both earth and sea alike. Night rushed down from heaven.
> East wind and south wind struck, and stormy west wind,
> and heaven-born north wind, rolling up great waves.[2]

He had a number of mortal sons, as well as merman Triton and shape-shifting Proteus. Triton was known for his ever-present conch shell, which he used as a horn; and in later life, Proteus turned into multiple sons who helped their father preside over the ocean. Poseidon's image has been used in artwork from statues to fountains, as in Rome's Trevi Fountain. Myths featuring Poseidon have been made into major motion pictures, such as *Jason and the Argonauts* and *Percy Jackson & the Olympians: The Lightning Thief*.

Proserpine (detail), Dante Gabriel Rossetti, 1874. The daughter of Demeter and Zeus, Persephone (Proserpine) was so lovely that she tempted the god of the Underworld himself, Hades, to kidnap her and keep her as his wife.

CHAPTER 3

The Kidnapping of Persephone

The Sirens had another possible beginning. It was told in the Homeric Hymn to Demeter, dating back to the end of the seventh or beginning of the sixth century BCE.

Once again, they began as sea nymphs. Their names and numbers change depending on who tells the story. Some say there were three, some four, some five or more. More than a dozen different names were given to the women, including Agalope (Beautiful Face), Molpe (Song), Parthenope (Maiden Voice), and Thelxioe (Charming Voice).

In this version of the myth, several of these singing sea nymphs were plucked from the sea by Demeter (DIH-mih-ter), sister of Zeus and sustainer of life and crops on earth. Her name means "Mother Earth." She chose the nymphs as protectors and playmates for her daughter by Zeus, Persephone (per-SEH-fuh-nee). In this job, they failed miserably.

Demeter adored her beautiful daughter. When Hades (HAY-deez), god of the Underworld, decided that he wanted her for his bride to help rule the dead, Zeus agreed to let him take her—without talking it over with either Demeter or Persephone. That proved to be a terrible idea.

One day, Persephone was out picking flowers with the sea nymphs. One particular flower drew her attention. It was covered in hundreds of brilliant blossoms. Hades had put it there to attract and trap her. As the young maiden reached for it, Hades appeared. Author Edith Hamilton describes her abduction:

The lord of the dark underworld, the king of the multitudinous dead, carried her off when, enticed by the
wondrous bloom of the narcissus, she strayed too far
from her companions. In his chariot, drawn by coal-
black steeds, he rose up through a chasm in the earth,
and grasping the maiden by the wrist set her beside
him. He bore her away weeping, down to the underworld. The high hills echoed her cry and the depths of
the sea, and her mother heard it.[1]

When Demeter realized that her daughter had been kidnapped,
she was furious. She began searching frantically for Persephone, but
to no avail. For nine days and nights, she looked everywhere. She
simply could not find her daughter. Finally, she turned to the nymphs
who were supposed to have been protecting Persephone. What happened next is not clear. In some stories, she gave the women wings
so that they could fly to faraway places in search of her. Other versions say she did it out of anger, as a lifelong curse for their neglect.
Some say that the women were suddenly shaped like birds except
for their heads. Others describe them as having women's bodies and
heads with bird wings. Different statues, vases, and other forms of art
show them in these forms, as well as several other combinations of
human and bird.

While Demeter searched and grieved for her daughter, the rest of
the world suffered. As Mother Earth, she was in charge of the health
and fertility of crops, animals, and people. Because of her grief,
everything began to wither and die. When Demeter went to Helios,
the sun god who saw everything, he revealed to her that it was Zeus
who had arranged for Hades to steal Persephone away. Demeter
was enraged. Zeus found out, and he knew something had to be
done.

He sent Hermes to negotiate for Persephone's return. By then,
however, Persephone had eaten some pomegranate seeds, which

The Rape of Persephone, Luca Giordano, 1684–1686. The Sirens could not protect Persephone when Hades kidnapped her.

indicated that she was willing to stay in the Underworld. She liked being a queen. Once she had eaten the seeds, she could not fully return to the world above. Instead, a compromise was reached. For four (or six) months of the year, she would serve as the queen of the dead with her husband. During this time, the earth above would descend into winter. Plants would shrivel up and die. Animals would

The Return of Persephone, Lord Frederic Leighton, 1891. Demeter joyfully welcomed her daughter back to the world each spring. No longer needed, the nymphs were sent away to the sea.

hibernate. Flowers would disappear as the sun hid behind clouds and cold spread throughout the land. When those months were over, however, she could return to live with her mother. This is when spring would arrive and the world would be born anew.

Persephone believed Hades was unlikely to be faithful to her. Indeed, when she discovered that he was having an affair with a beautiful water nymph named Menthe (MEN-thee), Persephone proceeded to walk all over her—literally. She turned Menthe into the plant that is known today as mint, then trampled her.

Once her daughter was home, Demeter had no more use for the nymphs. She banished them from the palace, to three rocky islands known as the *Sirenum scopuli*. These islands were thought to be located in the sea between Sicily and Italy. They were encircled by huge, sharp boulders, perfectly designed to wreck any ships that wandered too close, lured in by the Sirens' song.

The Sirens sat upon the rocks, singing and playing their instruments. The image of these women surrounded by the bleached white bones of their victims struck terror in the hearts of Greeks young and old.

Nymphs:
The Nature Spirits

As full of frightening, vicious monsters as many of the Greek myths were, they were also full of stories about beautiful nature spirits known as nymphs. Their origins are not clear. Most of them appeared to be former human women who came to an accidental end. In order to preserve their beauty, they were turned into nymphs. Others were the daughters of minor gods or goddesses. The Oceanids, for example, were the three thousand daughters of Oceanus, god of the ocean.

What kind of nymph a spirit was depended on where she lived. If she was near a river or spring, she was a Naiad. Mountain-dwelling nymphs were known as Oreads, while those in groves were Alseids. Hamadryads lived in the trees, and each type of tree had its own special nymph. For example, Orea lived in the ash tree, Ptelea in the elm, Carya in the nut tree, and Aegeirus in the poplar. Nymphs usually accompanied Artemis, goddess of the hunt, and they watched the flocks of Apollo and Hermes. The Hesperides were nymphs who guarded Hera's Golden Apples.

Some nymphs were kind and nurturing, such as those who saved Hephaestus (heh-FES-tus), god of the forge, after he was hurled from Olympus into the sea. Others were shown as cunning and sneaky. A nymph of a spring saw the beautiful Hylas and pulled him in so that she could keep him forever. Nymphs had the power to turn men into plants and animals as well.

Although nymphs could live a very long time, they were not immortal. Some of the best-known nymphs in Greek literature are Calypso, the nymph who kept Odysseus entertained for seven years; Harmonia, who gave birth to the Amazons; Eurydice, the wife of Orpheus; and Amalthea, the foster mother of Zeus.

Hylas and the Nymphs, John William Waterhouse, 1896. Hylas, squire of Hercules and an Argonaut, fell in love with the spring nymphs and was never heard from or seen again.

The Fisherman and the Siren, by Knut Ekvall (1843–1912). Many fishermen were lost to the tempting sounds of the Sirens, pulled under the surface of the water in the hopes of finally reaching these alluring women.

CHAPTER 4

Temptation of Jason and the Argonauts

Other than the tale of Odysseus, there are not many stories about the temptations of the Sirens. However, another famous voyager and his crew did run into these dangerous women. The captain's name was Jason, and his ship was *The Argo*. His crew members were known as the Argonauts (AR-goh-nots).

Jason had an unusual upbringing. His uncle Pelias (PEE-lee-us) stole the kingdom from Jason's father and would have killed the boy, but Jason's mother secretly sent him away to the Thessalian forest to be raised by Chiron (KY-ron), an old and wise centaur (half-horse, half-man). Chiron was a talented creature in everything from medicine and music to hunting and warfare. He taught a number of famous heroes, including Achilles.

As an adult, Jason returned to his homeland. Pelias panicked; he was not about to give up his kingdom. Instead, he sent Jason on what was considered an impossible quest. He was to find and bring home the Golden Fleece, the coat of a divine ram. He sent out a call for the bravest sailors to be his shipmates on the adventure. Those who responded included the musician Orpheus (OR-fee-us); the hero Heracles (HAYR-uh-kleez, whom the Romans called Hercules: HER-kyoo-leez); and Peleus, the father of Achilles.

An Impossible Mission

The voyage was full of danger and excitement. The men encountered Harpies, fierce flying creatures, as well as clashing rocks. When the Argonauts finally found the Golden Fleece, they could not get it from King Aeetes (eye-EE-teez) until they passed his test: Jason had to harness two vicious fire-breathing bulls, plow a field, sow it with seeds, and then reap the harvest—all in one day. It was a huge challenge, but help from a few goddesses made it possible. A salve protected Jason from the flames. When the seeds grew angry warriors instead of plants, Jason defeated them by throwing a stone at one. The men began fighting each other until all of them had perished.

Although the king said he would give Jason the fleece, he had lied. He had it nailed to a tree and guarded by a dragon. The king's daughter, however, slipped a sleeping potion to the creature and Jason escaped with the fleece. He had done the impossible!

On their triumphant journey home, Jason and the Argonauts had more adventures. One of them included sailing close to the islands where the Sirens lived. Fortunately, Jason had been told of the threat, and he was prepared. The music began to play, and it was more beautiful than he had expected. Claudianus, a theologian who lived in the fifth century CE, wrote of it:

> Sirens, sweet fruit of the sea, bird-maidens, lived among the Waves . . . .Their sacred music, gentle danger of the sea, was pleasurable terrors among the waves. On the keel of the ship lingered the caressing air, while from aft, a voice invaded the ship. But the seaman longed not to take the secure route home. But there was no pain; joy itself dealt death.[1]

As the Sirens' song began to be heard, Jason ordered Orpheus to begin singing and playing music on his lyre. Orpheus's music drowned out the sound of the Sirens, saving the lives of the Argonauts.

The Tale of Butes
The only person who did hear the alluring song was a sailor named Butes. He jumped overboard and began swimming to the women.

Jason's capture of the Golden Fleece was remarkable and unexpected. When he presented it to Pelias, everyone was amazed that he had survived.

Athena and her owl look on as Jason is swallowed by a dragon in this fifth century BCE cup kept at the Vatican Museum.

What happened to him at that point, once again, depends on which version of the story you read. In one, he is rescued from the water by the goddess Aphrodite. In another, he comes to quite a different end.

When he was just a small child, Butes was found by the nymph Cora (KOR-uh). He was raised by many nymphs, and as he grew into a handsome young man, all of them loved and wanted him for their own. They began to fight over him. Cora knew something had to be done before things got worse. She decided that Butes should be sent on a mission to Olympus to deliver honey, the nectar of the gods, to those above. This would give the boy time to mature and the nymphs time to find other mates.

A flask of honey was given to Butes, and he took it to the gods on Olympus. He was told to give it to any of the male gods he chose, but not to any of the female gods, as they would get jealous and begin to argue. Butes meant to follow orders, but when he laid eyes on Aphrodite, he forgot everything he had been told. He fell in love and gave the flask to her. As predicted, fighting broke out among the goddesses. To keep Butes safe, Aphrodite put a spell of protection on him. Although he was chased all night, Aphrodite made sure he remained safe. When angry goddesses closed in on him, she sent doves to surround him. Each one dropped a rose branch, which grew into wild, thick bushes covered in thorns. The goddesses could not get through. Then Aphrodite went to Zeus and told him that the goddesses were arguing—in direct disobedience to his rule. In response, Zeus sent down a lightning bolt and scared the goddesses away.

Athena was one of the goddesses who had chased Butes. She was jealous of Aphrodite, and so, to get back at the nymphs who had sent Butes, she turned them into bees. Cora, the queen bee, was given the ability to speak. When Butes returned home, she flew directly to him and warned him of Athena's anger. She told him to

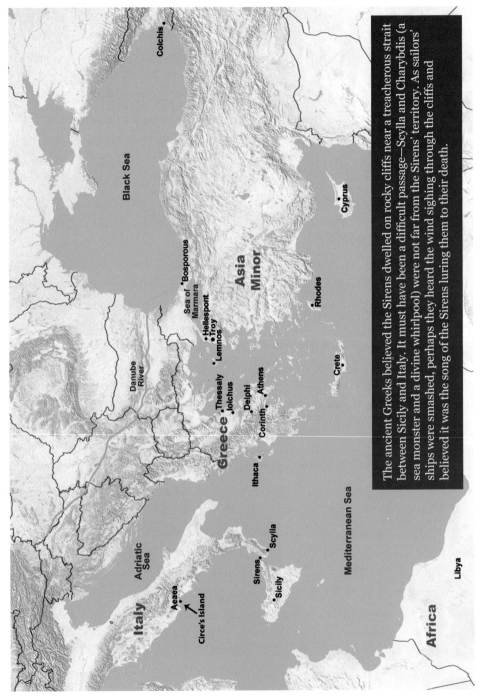

The ancient Greeks believed the Sirens dwelled on rocky cliffs near a treacherous strait between Sicily and Italy. It must have been a difficult passage—Scylla and Charybdis (a sea monster and a divine whirlpool) were not far from the Sirens' territory. As sailors' ships were smashed, perhaps they heard the wind sighing through the cliffs and believed it was the song of the Sirens luring them to their death.

go to sea and hope that Poseidon would protect him. He followed her advice and joined Jason on his ship as one of the Argonauts.

Athena could not be stopped that easily. She went to Circe and asked her to use the Sirens to lure *The Argo* close. However, she did not want the ship to crash on the rocks. Instead, Athena asked Circe to use her transformation spells to change all of the crew except Butes into hungry wolves. Circe agreed. She used a chariot pulled by

A replica of *The Argo*. According to Apollonius of Rhodes, author of *The Argonautica*, *The Argo* was built by a shipwright named Argus. It was believed that the goddess Hera watched over the ship and its sailors. The ship was dedicated to Poseidon.

owls to fly over the ship and cast her spell. The Sirens saw her and knew immediately what she was up to. They did not want to hurt the sailors, so they flew after the chariot, scaring away the owls. When the owls escaped, the chariot began to fall toward the sea. At the very last moment, Circe turned herself into a bat and flew back to the island.

As in the other story, Butes jumped from the ship and swam toward the Sirens, but instead of being rescued again by Aphrodite, the Sirens pulled him from the water before the man-eating jellyfish could get him. After he rested a bit, he had an idea. He asked the Sirens to fly him over the jellyfish so that he could look at it and see how it behaved. The Sirens grabbed him in their bird-like talons and, holding him firmly, flew low over the jellyfish. Once he understood, Butes asked them to fly over again, only lower. This time, he used his knife to cut the jellyfish. Soon it began eating itself. It grew smaller and smaller and finally disappeared completely, never to threaten another sailor.

Poseidon found out what Butes had done and was grateful. He sent Proteus—now forgiven for helping Athena and back to working for his father—to rescue Butes. Butes was thankful and had only one request: to turn Cora and the others back into nymphs.

When he found out that it was impossible and that the love of his life would remain a bee, he asked Poseidon to turn him into a bee also. His wish was granted, and he flew back to live the rest of his days with Cora.

Statue of a Siren holding a tortoise-shell lyre, fourth century BCE. In some myths, Sirens were part woman and part bird, while in other stories, they took different shapes.

The Music of Orpheus

Although Orpheus was well known for his ability to make enchanting music, it was the death of his young bride, a nymph named Eurydice (yuh-RIH-dih-kee), that brought his greatest challenge.

The two had just been married when Eurydice was bitten by a snake. The venom killed her. Orpheus was so grief-stricken that he quit playing instruments. He quit singing. Finally, he decided that he had to go after Eurydice in the Underworld. He knew the journey could prove fatal, but it was a risk he was willing to take if he could bring back his wife.

Orpheus used his music first to charm Charon (KAYR-on) to take him across the river Styx and then to fool Cerberus (SER-ber-us), the guard dog, into letting him into the Underworld. Finally, he had to face Hades and Persephone and convince them to let him take Eurydice back. His pleas—and his soothing music—worked. Hades told him that he could have his wife back on one condition: he was not to look at her until they were both out of the Underworld. Orpheus agreed to the terms, but the temptation to steal a glance at his beloved wife proved too much for him. Just before they reached the surface, he looked back at Eurydice. As he did, her image faded, and she returned to the Underworld.

Lost without Eurydice, Orpheus was torn to pieces by Maenads, or madwomen. When they were finished with him, only his head was left. It floated downstream, constantly calling Eurydice's name. Later, his head became an oracle, and people asked it for help on important questions.

Orpheus and Eurydice, by Christian Kratzenstein-Stub, 1783–1816. One look back at his loved one was enough to condemn Eurydice to the Underworld and Orpheus to death.

Calliope, by Marcello Bacciarelli, eighteenth century. Calliope is one of the many muses mentioned in countless myths. Like her sisters, she was the source of art and many types of music. The steam organ—an instrument often heard at the circus—is named for her.

CHAPTER 5

Sirens, Muses, and Music

In mythology, little is told of the Sirens other than their role as Persephone's protectors and their encounters with Jason and his ship and Odysseus and his crew. A Roman marble piece from the third century does hint that another story took place, however. In it Athena, Zeus, and Hera (HAYR-uh) are shown as judges at a music contest between the Muses and the Sirens. Apparently Hera, queen of the gods, convinced the Sirens to compete with the Muses.

Meet the Muses

The nine Muses were all the daughters of Zeus. They were talented goddesses who inspired others to write poetry, compose music, and perform dances. They also inspired philosophers and scientists. In fact, their name is in today's words *music* and *museum*. Hesiod wrote of them:

> They are all of one mind, their hearts are set upon song and their spirit is free from care. He is happy whom the Muses love. For though a man has sorrow and grief in his soul, yet when the servant of the Muses sings, at once he forgets his dark thoughts and remembers not his troubles. Such is the holy gift of the Muses to men.[1]

Calliope (kah-LY-oh-pee) was the oldest of the Muses. Her name means "beautiful music," and she was known for her ability to negotiate arguments between the gods. She was considered the muse of epic poetry.

Minerva and the Muses, painted by Jacques Stella, seventeenth century. The Muses gave inspiration to others in the form of music, art, poetry, and more. They were beautiful and talented, but also prone to anger if their skills were ever challenged.

Clio (KLEE-oh, "Renown") was the muse of history. Later, she was credited with introducing one of Greece's first alphabets.

Erato (ayr-AH-toh, "Loveliness") was the muse of poetry about love and passion, while **Euterpe** (yoo-TER-pee, "Gladness") was the muse of music and lyric poetry.

Melpomene (mel-POH-muh-nee, "Singer") was the muse of tragedy, and **Polymnia** (pah-LIM-nee-uh, "Many Songs") was the muse of sacred hymns or songs addressing the gods.

Terpsichore (terp-SIH-kuh-ree, "Delighting in the Dance") was the muse of dance. In some versions of the myths, she is listed as the mother of the Sirens.

Thalia (THAY-lee-uh, "Good Cheer") was the muse of comedy, the opposite of Melpomene, while **Urania** (yuh-RAY-nee-uh, "Heavenly One") was the muse of astronomy and astrology.

How the music contest between the Muses and the Sirens began depends, once again, on who tells the story. For example, some versions say it was the Sirens who came up with the idea. Others say it was the Muses. Still others say it was the wrath of Hera.

The Muses had been challenged to contests before. The nine daughters of King Pierus (py-AYR-us) were extremely proud of their musical skills, and whenever mortals grew too boastful, the gods tended to do something to humble them. The daughters decided to compete against the Muses to see which group was more talented. The competition took place at Mount Helicon. When the mortals began to sing, so the story goes, the sky grew dark and stormy. Fog rolled in. When the Muses began singing, however, blue sky and sunshine returned and nature rejoiced. The gods declared the Muses the winners, and Pierus's daughters were turned into birds as punishment for challenging them.

The Sirens were sure that their musical abilities were better than anyone else's, and so once again, the Muses were challenged. As the two groups sang, it became clear that while the Muses' songs were designed to inspire and encourage others to find creativity, the Sirens' songs were designed to deceive and lure people to their death. When the Sirens lost, the Muses punished them by plucking out all of their feathers and wearing them in their crowns.

Music of Ancient Greece

Music was an important element in Greek culture. Learning to play at least one instrument was considered essential to a person's education. Music inspired people to paint, draw, dance, sing, and perform other arts. Harps, flutes, and panpipes called syringes (singular: *syrinx*) were well known in myths. Perhaps the most common instrument was the lyre, a guitar-like instrument made with a tortoise shell having three to twelve strings. It was supposedly invented by Hermes and given to Apollo, the god of music, who wanted to learn how to play it.

Apollo and Marsyas, by Pietro di Cristoforo Vannucci (1450–1523). Marsyas (left) challenged the god to a music contest and tragically lost.

Later, Apollo played the lyre in a contest with Marsyas, who played the pipes. He also challenged the goat-god Pan in a musical contest. Only Midas thought Pan was the better player, and for his poor judgment, Apollo awarded him with the ears of an ass.

Cymbals are mentioned in a Homeric Hymn to Apollo, and Hercules used a set of castanets for scaring a flock of fierce birds in one of his twelve labors. Being able to produce music—whether with an instrument or simply one's voice—was considered a necessary skill for the Greeks, whether one was a Siren, god, or otherwise.

F.Y.I.
FOR YOUR INFORMATION

The Sirens in
Today's World

The Sirens still exist in today's world in some ways. A woman who lures a man into trouble is often referred to as a siren. Flirts or wild female celebrities are sometimes labeled as sirens.

The 2000 movie *O Brother, Where Art Thou?* starring George Clooney, Holly Hunter, and John Turturro, was based on Homer's *Odyssey*. Both tales recount the story of a man trying to get home and running into obstacles along the way. Many of the characters' names in the movie are based on the gods and mortals, including Everett Ulysses McGill (played by Clooney), Menelaus O'Daniel (played by Charles Durning), Tiresias (played by Lee Weaver), and Penelope (played by Holly Hunter). Certain characters in the movie also mirror Polyphemus, the Cyclops (a one-eyed Bible salesman), and other creatures. Some washerwomen in the movie are compared to sirens because they lure men to a river.

The Sirens have been found in more works than the Greek and Roman myths. They have appeared in the writings of James Joyce, H.G. Wells, Oscar Wilde, and William Butler Yeats. In addition, their images have appeared in famous paintings, statues, fountains, and other art.

In Coney Island, New York, there is an annual Siren Music Festival, and a number of different musical groups have called themselves Sirens. In 1993, the movie *Sirens*, starring Hugh Grant and Sam Neill, focused on the story of three young women tempting husbands and wives to leave their marriages. There is also an annual conference dedicated to female authors of fantasy literature called Sirens.

Of course, the noisy piece of equipment on emergency vehicles that screams out to warn of trouble is also called a siren. One author writes about that connection, saying, "Since the First World War, perched atop churches and city towers, they [sirens] have been warning of the arrival of a new breed of death-bearing birds. In the event of disaster sirens start automatically. Could that be the only way they have left to continue their chant, whatever it may be, in the stubborn hope that someone might hear?"[2]

Chapter 1. Facing the Siren Song
1. Homer, *The Odyssey*, translated by E. V. Rieu (New York: Penguin Classics, 2010), Book 10, lines 388–399.
2. Ibid., Book 12, lines 39–46.

Chapter 2. An Ongoing Feud
1. Homer, *The Iliad*, translated by E.V. Rieu (New York: Penguin Classics, 2003), Book 14, lines 153–160.
2. Ibid.

Chapter 3. The Kidnapping of Persephone
1. Edith Hamilton, *Mythology* (New York: Grand Central Publishing, 1942), p. 51.

Chapter 4. Temptation of Jason and the Argonauts
1. Meri Lao, *Sirens: Symbols of Seduction* (Rochester, VT: Inner Traditions International, 1999), p. 53.

Chapter 5. Sirens, Muses, and Music
1. Edith Hamilton, *Mythology* (New York: Grand Central Publishing, 1942), p. 37.
2. Meri Lao, *Sirens: Symbols of Seduction* (Rochester, VT: Inner Traditions International, 1999), p. 178.

Odysseus and the Sirens, unknown artist, nineteenth century CE

THE SIRENS

Books

Golding, Julia. *The Companions Quartet: Secret of the Sirens*. Tarrytown, NY: Marshall Cavendish, 2007.

Jolley, Dan. *Graphic Myths and Legends: Odysseus: Escaping Poseidon's Curse*. Minneapolis: Graphic Universe, 2008.

Lawrence, Caroline. *The Sirens of Surrentum*. New York: Roaring Brook Press, 2007.

Riordan, James. *Jason and the Golden Fleece*. London: Frances Lincoln Children's Books, 2005.

Schulte, Mary. *The Sirens*. San Diego: KidHaven Press, 2007.

Ursu, Anne. *The Siren Song*. New York: Atheneum, 2008.

Works Consulted

Apollodorus. *The Library*. Translated by J. G. Frazer. Loeb Classical Library, Volumes 121 & 122. Cambridge, MA: Harvard University Press; London: William Heinemann Ltd., 1921. http://www.theoi.com/Text/Apollodorus1.html

Apollonius. *The Argonautica*. Translated by R. C. Seaton. Internet Classics Archive. http://classics.mit.edu/Apollonius/argon.4.iv.html

Bulfinch, Thomas. *Myths of Greece and Rome*. New York: Penguin Books, 1979.

Cotterell, Arthur. *Classical Mythology*. New York: Lorenz Books, 2000.

Hamilton, Edith. *Mythology*. New York: Grand Central Publishing, 1942.

Hesiod. *The Homeric Hymns and Homerica*. English Translation by Hugh G. Evelyn-White. Cambridge, MA: Harvard University Press; London: William Heinemann Ltd., 1914.

Homer. *The Iliad*. Translated by E. V. Rieu. New York: Penguin Classics, 2003.

———. *The Odyssey*. Translated by E. V. Rieu. New York: Penguin Classics, 2010.

Lao, Meri. *Sirens: Symbols of Seduction*. Rochester, VT: Inner Traditions International, 1999.

March, Jenny. *Cassell's Dictionary of Classical Mythology*. London: Cassell & Co., 2001.

———. *The Penguin Book of Classical Myths*. New York: Penguin Books, 2008.

Pausanias. *Description of Greece*. Translated by W.H.S. Jones. Classical E-Text. http://www.theoi.com/Text/Pausanias8B.html

FURTHER READING

On the Internet
Greek Mythology Link: Sirens
    http://homepage.mac.com/cparada/GML/SIRENS.html
Sirens
    http://www.theoi.com/Pontios/Seirenes.html
Sirens: World Mythology
    http://www.kidzworld.com/article/1850-sirens

Ligeia Siren, by Dante Gabriel Rossetti, 1873

PHOTO CREDITS: Cover, p. 1—Sir Edward John Poynter; pp. 6, 9, 18, 27, 43—John William Waterhouse; p. 11—Herbert James Draper; p. 13—Nicholas Monsiau; pp. 14, 17, 20, 21, 31, 32, 44—CreativeCommons; pp. 22, 46—Dante Gabriel Rossetti; p. 25—Luca Giordano; p. 26—Lord Frederic Leighton; p. 28—Knut Ekvall; p. 34—Carly Peterson; p. 35—G. Ganotopoulos; p. 37—Christian Kratzenstein-Stub; p. 38—Marcello Bacciarelli; p. 40—Jacques Stella; p. 42— Pietro di Cristoforo Vannucci. Every effort has been made to locate all copyright holders of material used in this book. If any errors or omissions have occurred, corrections will be made in future editions of this book.

GLOSSARY

abduction (ab-DUK-shun)—Taking someone against his or her will.

castanets (kas-teh-NETS)—Hand-held musical instruments, usually made of shells, wood, or metal, that make a loud noise when banged together.

epic (EH-pik) **poetry**—A long story of a legendary hero told in the form of a poem.

immortality (ih-mor-TAL-ih-tee)—The ability to live forever.

keel—A long board or bead under a boat or ship that extends from the front to the rear; it helps keep the boat upright and going in a straight line.

lyric (LEER-ik) **poetry**—Poetry that can be set to music, especially to the music of a lyre, and that has strong emotion.

mortal (MOR-tul)—A human; a being with a definite lifespan.

multitudinous (mul-tih-TOO-dih-nus)—Having a large number of individuals.

negotiate (neh-GOH-shee-ayt)—To help two arguing parties reach an agreement.

nymph (NIMF)—Any of the minor nature deities that lived in the mountains, streams, trees, or other natural settings.

Oceanid (oh-shee-AN-id)—Any of the three thousand daughters of Oceanus; nymphs who lived in the ocean.

oracle (OR-uh-kul)—A priest or priestess who gives predictions or advice; the ancient Greeks believed oracles spoke for a god.

pomegranate (PAH-muh-gran-it)—A tart red berry about the size of an apple filled with seeds encased in individual juicy cells.

strait (STRAYT)—A narrow passage of water connecting two larger bodies of water.

suitor (SOO-tur)—Someone who courts a woman in order to marry her.

theologian (thee-oh-LOH-jun)—Someone who studies theology (religion).

transform (trans-FORM)—To change shape.

trident (TRY-dent)—A three-pronged spear; it is the symbol of Poseidon (Neptune).

THE SIRENS